U0052912

For Shiney

我討厭寫作業

I HATE HOMEWORK

文🖐Jill McDougall

圖🖐余麗婷

"I hate homework," says Red Nose after school.

"It's not so bad," says Purple Toes.

Red Nose runs to the TV.

"Wait!" says Ma *Monster.

"What?" says Red Nose.

"Do your homework," says Ma.

Red Nose takes out her pens. She takes out her ruler. She takes out her books. She looks at the *blank TV. "I hate homework," she says sadly.

The next day, Red Nose runs home. She hides her school bag under her bed. Then she *puts on the TV.

"Wait!" says Ma Monster.

"What?" says Red Nose.

"Do your homework," says Ma.

"I can't," says Red Nose. "I've lost my school bag."

Ma goes out of the room. She comes back with the school bag. "Here," says Ma. "Now you can do your homework."

Red Nose takes out her pens. She takes out her ruler. She takes out her books. She looks at the blank TV. "I hate homework," she says sadly.

The next day, Red Nose sees a *note from Ma.

It says:

"Oh no!" says Red Nose. "I hate homework."

"It's not so bad," says Purple Toes.

Red Nose goes into her room. Then she climbs out the window.

"What are you doing?" asks Purple Toes.

"I am putting my bag on the *roof," says Red Nose. "Ma won't find it there."

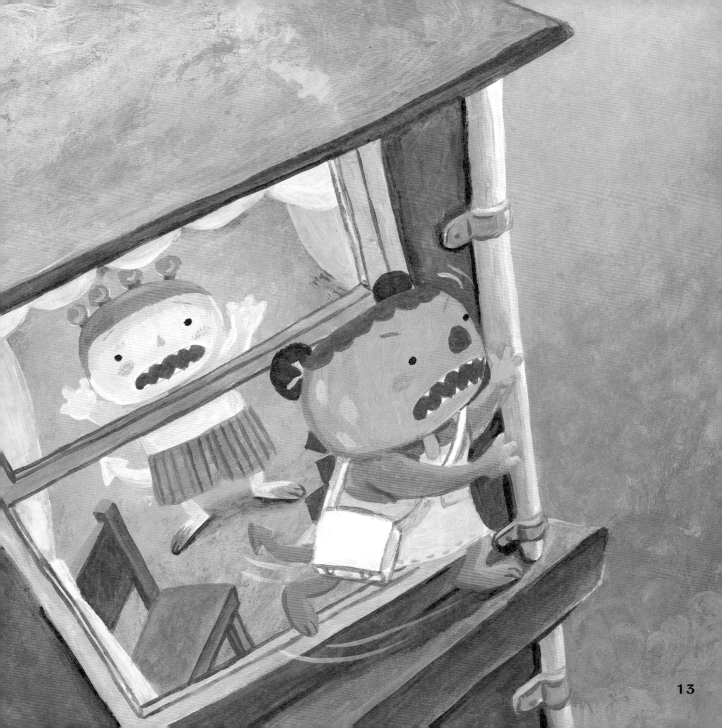

She climbs onto the roof.

"Come down," *yells Purple Toes.

"Okay," says Red Nose. Then she says, "I can't get down."

"What?"

"I can't get down. I'm *stuck."

"I'll get a *ladder," says Purple Toes. He runs off.

Soon he is up on the roof with Red Nose. "Now you can come down," he says.

But the ladder starts to *shake.

Then it *slides...slides...slides... *all the way

down to the ground.

"Oh no!" says Purple Toes. "Now we are both stuck on the roof."

"Ma will be home soon," says Red Nose. "Let's sing a song."

The little monsters sing a song. Then they sing another song. Ma is still not home.

"What can we do now?" asks Red Nose.

"We can do your homework," says Purple Toes.

Red Nose takes out her pens. She takes out her ruler. She takes out her books.

"I hate homework," she says.

"Why?"

"We always have *sums," said Red Nose. "Sums are hard."

"I'll help you," says Purple Toes. "You can use your ruler to *work out the sums."

"Oh," says Red Nose. "That's not so hard."

Red Nose works out a sum on her ruler. Then she works out another sum on her ruler.

Soon Ma comes home. She helps the little monsters get down.

Red Nose runs to the TV.

28

"Wait!" says Ma Monster.

"What?" says Red Nose.

"Do your homework," says Ma.

"I've done it," says Red Nose.

"You have?" says Ma. "But you hate homework."

Red Nose smiles at Purple Toes. "It's not so bad," she says.

"Good," says Ma. "Then you can do your *chores."

"Oh no!" says Red Nose. She looks sadly at the blank TV. "I **HATE** chores!"

生_{ㄕㄥ}字_{ㄗˋ}表_{ㄅㄧㄠˇ}

p. 19 shake [ʃek] *v.* 搖動、搖晃

slide [slaɪd] *v.* 滑動、滑行

all the way 一路到底、全程的

p. 24 sum [sʌm] *n.* 算術題

work out 計算

p. 32 chore [tʃor] *n.* 家中的雜務

（詞性以縮寫表示：*n.* 名詞，*adj.* 形容詞，*v.* 動詞）

我討厭寫作業

放學後，紅鼻子說：「我討厭寫作業。」

紫腳趾說：「沒有那麼糟啦。」

紅鼻子跑到電視前面。

怪獸媽媽說：「等一下！」

紅鼻子說：「怎麼了？」

媽媽說：「去寫妳的作業。」

紅鼻子拿出她的筆，拿
出她的尺，再拿出她的
書。她看著沒有畫面的電視機，難過的
說：「我討厭寫作業。」

第二天，紅鼻子跑回家。她把書包藏到床底下，然後打開電視。

怪獸媽媽說：「等一下！」

紅鼻子說：「怎麼了？」

媽媽說：「去寫妳的作業。」

紅鼻子說：「我沒辦法寫作業，因為我的書包不見了。」

媽媽走出電視間，回來時手上拿著紅鼻子的書包。

她說：「拿去，現在妳可以寫作業了。」

紅鼻子拿出她的筆，拿出她的尺，再拿出她的書。她看著沒有畫面的電視機，難過的說：「我討厭寫作業。」

隔天，紅鼻子看到媽媽留了一
張紙條，上面寫著：
我去商店買東西。
記得要寫作業。

紅鼻子說:「喔，不！我討厭寫作業。」

紫腳趾說:「沒那麼糟啦。」

紅鼻子走進自己的房間，然後
爬出窗外。

紫腳趾問:「妳在做什麼?」

紅鼻子說:「我要把書包放到屋
頂上，這樣媽媽就找不到它了。」

她爬上屋頂。

紫腳趾大喊：「快下來！」

紅鼻子說：「好啦。」然後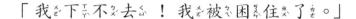

她說：「我下不去。」

「什麼？」

「我下不去！我被困住了。」

紫腳趾說：「我去拿梯子。」然後就跑走了。

很快的，他爬上屋頂和紅鼻子一起。他

說：「現在妳可以下去了。」

但是梯子卻開始搖晃了起來，然後它慢慢

的滑呀滑、滑呀滑、滑呀滑，一路滑到地

上。

紫腳趾說：「喔，糟了！現在我們兩個都被

困在屋頂上了。」

紅鼻子說：「媽媽很快就回來了，我們來唱

首歌吧。」

兩隻小怪獸唱了一首歌，接著又唱了另一

首，但媽媽還是沒有回來。

紅鼻子問：「我們現在能做什

麼呢？」

紫腳趾說：「我們可以做妳的

回家作業啊！」

紅鼻子拿出她的筆，拿出她的尺，再拿出

她的書。

她說：「我討厭寫作業。」

「為什麼？」

紅鼻子說：「我們總是有算術題，算術很難耶。」

紫腳趾說：「我來幫妳，妳可以用你的尺來

算出答案啊。」

紅鼻子說:「喔，其實不會太難。」

紅鼻子用尺算了一題算術，然後
她又用尺算了另外一題。

過了不久，媽媽回來了。她把兩隻
小怪獸救了下來，然後紅鼻子跑到
電視機前面。

怪獸媽媽說:「等一下!」

紅鼻子說:「怎麼了?」

媽媽說:「去寫妳的作業。」

紅鼻子說:「我已經寫完了。」

媽媽說:「妳寫完了?但是妳不是討厭寫作
業嗎?」

紅鼻子對著紫腳趾露出微笑，然後說:「其實沒那麼糟啦。」

媽媽說:「太好了，那妳現在可以做些家事。」

紅鼻子說:「喔，不!」她難過的看著沒有畫面的電視機，說:「我討厭做家事!」

文字迷宮解答：

								6.p		
1.e	4.r	a	s	e	r			e		
	u							n		7.b
	l	2.p	r	o	5.t	r	a	c	t	o	r
	e				r		i		o
	r				i		l		k
					a				
					n				
					g				
	3.p	e	n	c	i	l	b	o	x
					e				

45

文ㄨㄣˊ具ㄐㄩˋ總ㄗㄨㄥˇ動ㄉㄨㄥˋ員ㄩㄢˊ

紅ㄏㄨㄥˊ鼻ㄅㄧˊ子ㄗ (Red Nose) 最ㄗㄨㄟˋ討ㄊㄠˇ厭ㄧㄢˋ寫ㄒㄧㄝˇ作ㄗㄨㄛˋ業ㄧㄝˋ了ㄌㄜ。有ㄧㄡˇ一ㄧˋ天ㄊㄧㄢ在ㄗㄞˋ屋ㄨ頂ㄉㄧㄥˇ上ㄕㄤˋ，她ㄊㄚ試ㄕˋ著ㄓㄜ算ㄙㄨㄢˋ數ㄕㄨˋ學ㄒㄩㄝˊ，而ㄦˊ書ㄕㄨ包ㄅㄠ裡ㄌㄧˇ的ㄉㄜ文ㄨㄣˊ具ㄐㄩˋ通ㄊㄨㄥ通ㄊㄨㄥ出ㄔㄨ動ㄉㄨㄥˋ來ㄌㄞˊ幫ㄅㄤ忙ㄇㄤˊ，請ㄑㄧㄥˇ聽ㄊㄧㄥ CD 的ㄉㄜ第ㄉㄧˋ四ㄙˋ首ㄕㄡˇ，跟ㄍㄣ著ㄓㄜ一ㄧˋ起ㄑㄧˇ唸ㄋㄧㄢˋ，看ㄎㄢˋ看ㄎㄢˋ他ㄊㄚ們ㄇㄣ是ㄕˋ誰ㄕㄟˊ吧ㄅㄚ！

eraser
橡ㄒㄧㄤˋ皮ㄆㄧˊ擦ㄘㄚ

pencil
鉛ㄑㄧㄢ筆ㄅㄧˇ

book
書ㄕㄨ

ruler
尺ㄔˇ

school bag
書ㄕㄨ包ㄅㄠ

pencil box
鉛ㄑㄧㄢ筆ㄅㄧˇ盒ㄏㄜˊ

紅鼻子的書包裡還有其他文具喔

compass
圓規

scissor
剪刀

triangle
三角板

pen
原子筆

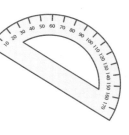

protractor
量角器

glue
膠水

WORD PUZZLE 文字迷宮

哇！白色的小方格是怎麼回事？其實紅鼻子的文具都躲在裡面，他們變成英文單字躺在方格裡，有的躺橫的，有的躺直的。請依照下面的提示，把這些單字找出來。

提示

* 這些字有：eraser, pencil, book, triangle, ruler, protractor, pencil box，每一個單字都有標數字，對照上面的數字和下面的描述，答案很快就出來了。

橫的：

1. 當你寫錯字的時候，必須用到它把錯字擦乾淨。
2. 做數學習題的時候，有時得靠它來量度數。
3. 把鉛筆、橡皮擦放在這個盒子裡，就不會不見了。

直的：

4. 畫線要用到它，線才會很直。
5. 它是三角形，可用來畫直角。
6. 它是一種筆，用它寫的字可以用橡皮擦擦掉。
7. 你的作業題目都在這個上面。

· 答案請參考第 45 頁

作者簡介

JILL MCDOUGALL lives in a cottage by the sea in South Australia. She has been a writer ever since she could hold a pencil and has written over ninety books for children. Her stories and poems are published in countries all around the world from the USA to Sweden to South Africa. Jill is also a teacher, an animal lover and a keen organic gardener.

Jill 目前住在澳洲南部海邊的一棟小屋裡。從她學會握筆的時候，她就是一位作家了，而她寫給兒童的作品已經超過九十本。從美國到瑞典，甚至南非，都能看到她出版的詩作及故事。Jill 同時也是一位老師、動物愛好者和愛好有機作物的園藝家。

繪者簡介

余麗婷 為自由插畫家，作品常見於國語日報、聯合報等，自寫自畫《家有怪物》曾獲第四屆國語日報牧笛獎。非常喜歡拍照和旅行。

她用壓克力顏料創作小怪獸系列，認為怪獸世界是充滿無限想像的。最想知道怪獸要怎麼用三隻爪子來蓋房子；最想把怪獸的爪子拿來做成餅乾造型，然後暢銷全世界。

Monster Series 小怪獸系列

學習英文0～2年者（國小1～3年級）適讀

世界上真的有怪獸嗎？
雖然他們有像恐龍一樣突起的的背脊
和尖尖的牙齒，
但是他們卻有一顆善良的心——
紅鼻子怪獸收留了鄰居的小貓，
紫腳趾怪獸教妹妹寫作業，
電視壞掉了，卻發現更有趣的事⋯⋯

一起來探索怪獸的世界吧！

—— 小怪獸系列有三本，皆附中英雙語CD ——

1. The TV Is Mine!
電視是我的！

2. I Hate Homework
我討厭寫作業

3. A Monster Surprise
小怪獸的驚喜

文／Jill McDougall
圖／余麗婷

國家圖書館出版品預行編目資料

I Hate Homework:我討厭寫作業 / Jill McDougall著;余
麗婷繪.－－初版一刷.－－臺北市：三民，2007
    面； 公分.－－(Fun心讀雙語叢書.小怪獸系列)
中英對照
ISBN 978－957－14－4681－3 (精裝)

1.英國語言－讀本

523.38   95025208

© I Hate Homework
——我討厭寫作業

著 作 人	Jill McDougall
繪　　者	余麗婷
責任編輯	曾鐘誼
美術設計	葉佩菱
發 行 人	劉振強
著作財產權人	三民書局股份有限公司
發 行 所	三民書局股份有限公司
	地址　臺北市復興北路386號
	電話　(02)25006600
	郵撥帳號　0009998-5
門 市 部	(復北店)臺北市復興北路386號
	(重南店)臺北市重慶南路一段61號
出版日期	初版一刷　2007年1月
編　　號	S 806911
定　　價	新臺幣壹佰玖拾元整

行政院新聞局登記證局版臺業字第○二○○號

有著作權‧不准侵害

ISBN　978-957-14-4681-3　(精裝)

http://www.sanmin.com.tw　三民網路書店